D1685634

Who Chomps with These Teeth?

by Cari Meister

60000483378

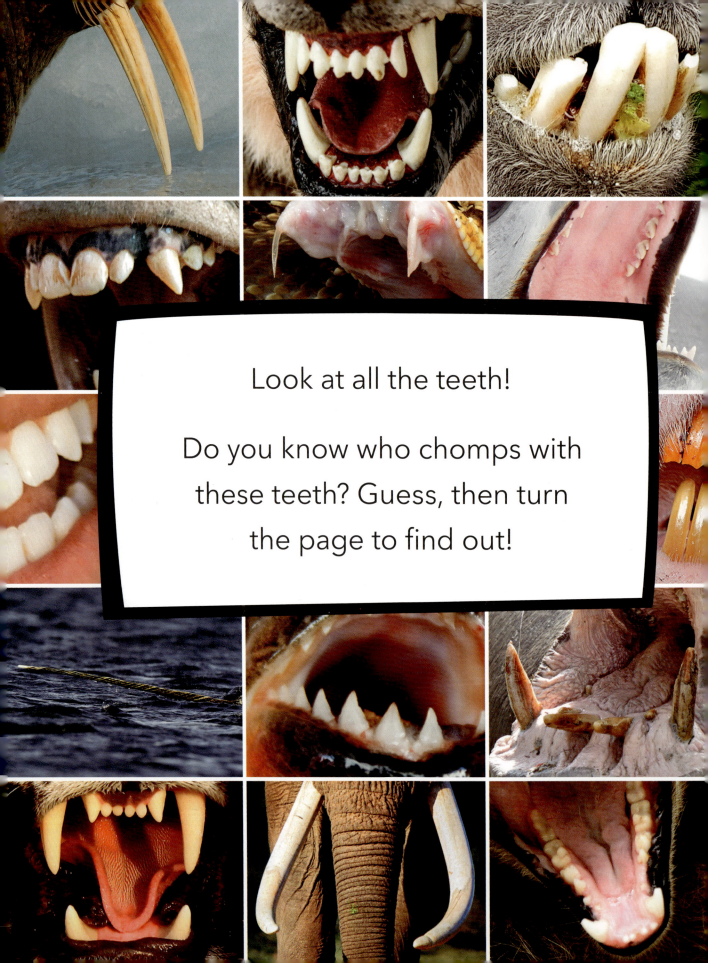

Look at all the teeth!

Do you know who chomps with these teeth? Guess, then turn the page to find out!

Who chomps with these teeth?

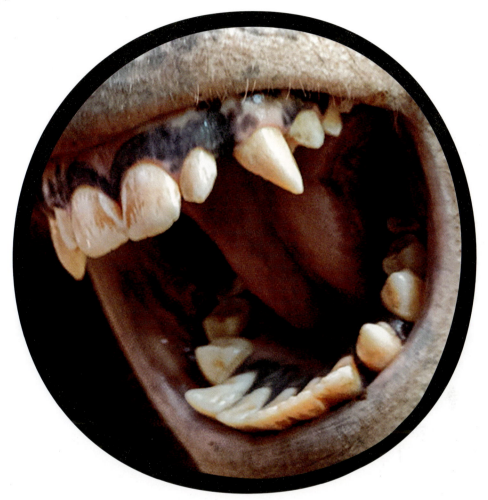

Turn and see!

ORANGUTAN

Smile! Like humans, orangutans have 32 teeth.

Who chomps with these teeth?

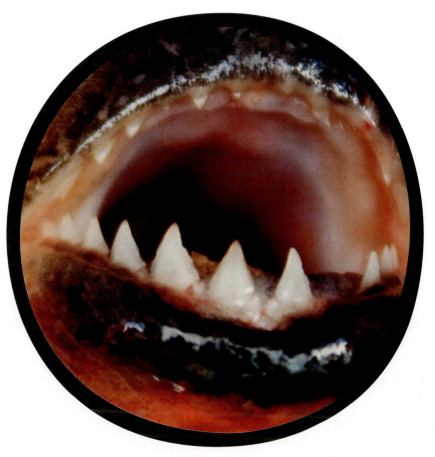

Turn and see!

PIRANHA

Sharp piranha teeth
are used for hunting.
Piranhas hunt in groups.

Who chomps with these teeth?

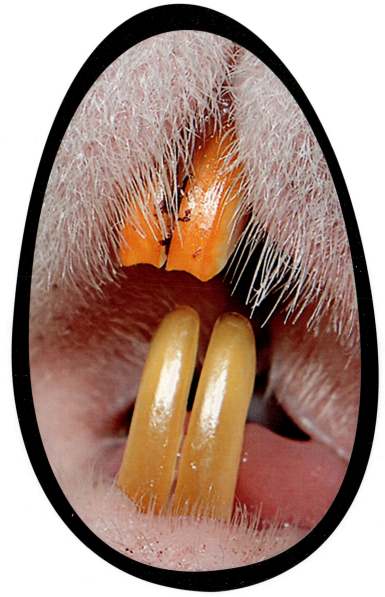

Turn and see!

RAT

A rat's teeth never stop growing.
All the better to eat CHEESE with!

Who uses this tooth?

Turn and see!

NARWHAL

A narwhal's long tooth is like a tusk. It is used to surprise prey.

Who chomps with these teeth?

Turn and see!

WOLF

Fierce teeth are a warning to other animals. Stay away from a wolf!

Who chomps with these teeth?

Turn and see!

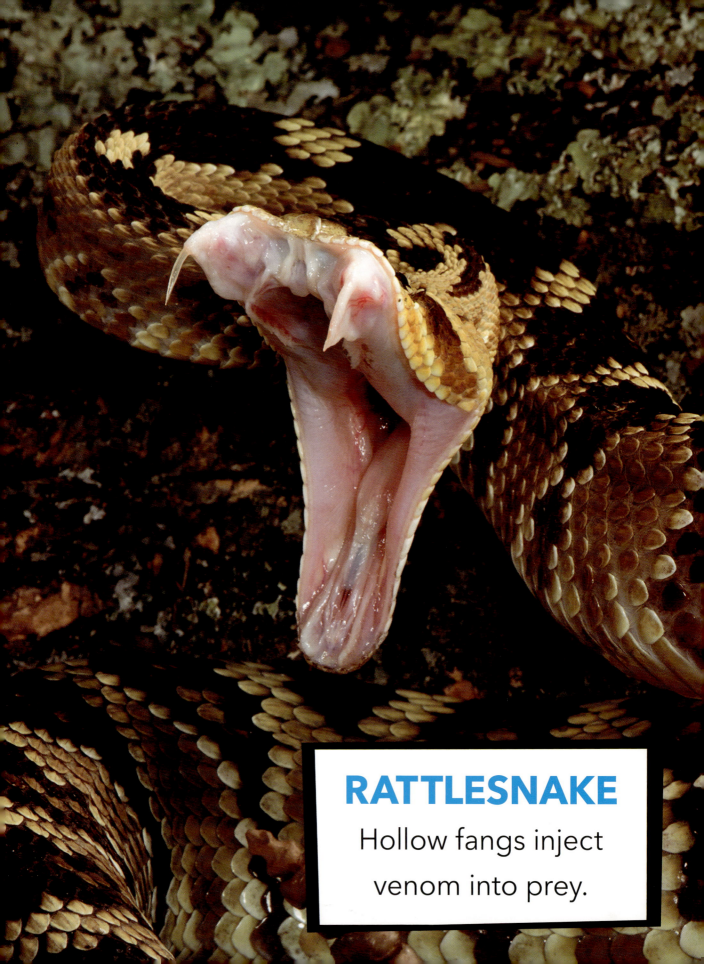

RATTLESNAKE

Hollow fangs inject venom into prey.

Who chomps with these teeth?

Turn and see!

HIPPOPOTAMUS

A hippo has the longest teeth of any land animal.

Who chomps with these teeth?

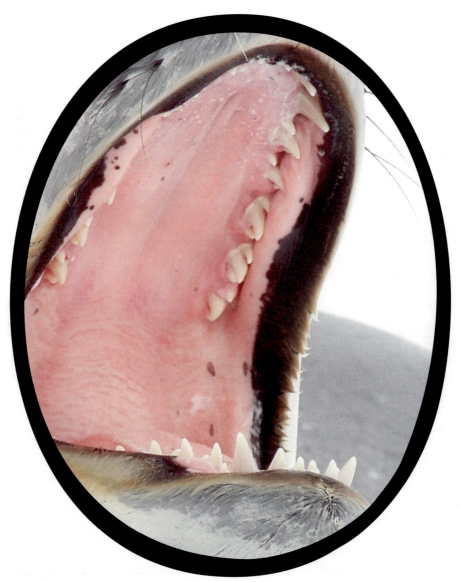

Turn and see!

LEOPARD SEAL

This seal's razor-sharp teeth easily grab and eat food.

Who chomps with these teeth?

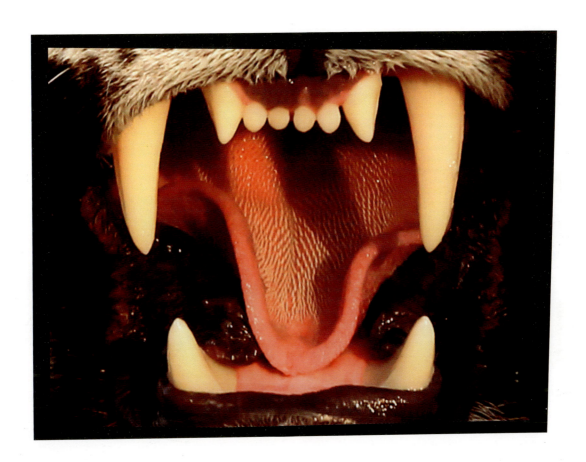

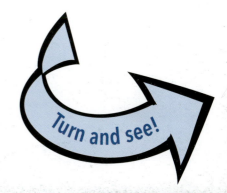

Turn and see!

TIGER

Long, sharp teeth are helpful when fighting other tigers.

Who uses these teeth?

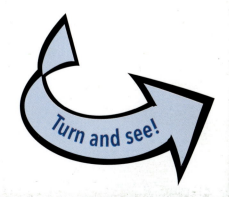
Turn and see!

WALRUS

Long ivory teeth called tusks help a walrus to pull its heavy body onto ice.

Who chomps with these teeth?

Turn and see!

LLAMA

Llamas use their teeth
for chewing grass.

Who chomps with these teeth?

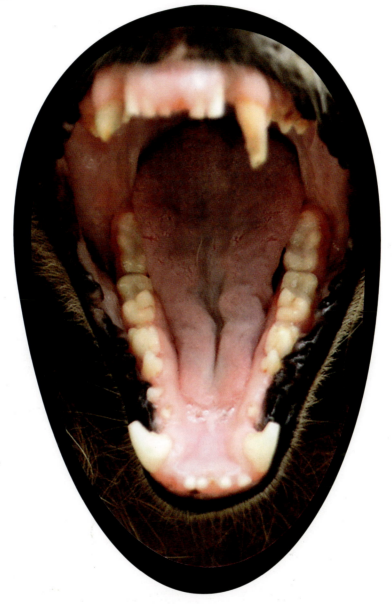

Turn and see!

RACCOON

A raccoon uses its teeth to nibble tasty fruit.

Who uses these teeth?

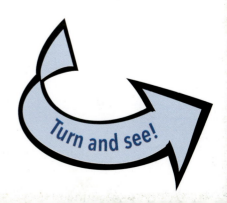

Turn and see!

ELEPHANT

Long elephant teeth become tusks. They dig and find water.

Who chomps with these teeth?

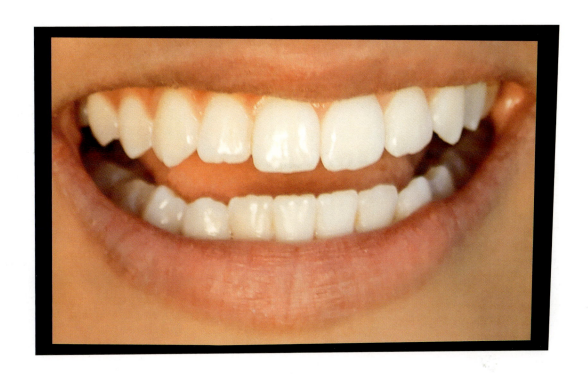

Turn and see!

HUMAN

Strong teeth help a child bite into a crunchy apple. Yum!

Teeth help animals to grab, dig and chomp. They are tools and weapons. Teeth are amazing!

Raintree is an imprint of Capstone Global Library Limited, a company incorporated in England and Wales having its registered office at 264 Banbury Road, Oxford, OX2 7DY – Registered company number: 6695582

www.raintree.co.uk
myorders@raintree.co.uk

Text © Capstone Global Library Limited 2021
The moral rights of the proprietor have been asserted.

All rights reserved. No part of this publication may be reproduced in any form or by any means (including photocopying or storing it in any medium by electronic means and whether or not transiently or incidentally to some other use of this publication) without the written permission of the copyright owner, except in accordance with the provisions of the Copyright, Designs and Patents Act 1988 or under the terms of a licence issued by the Copyright Licensing Agency, 5th Floor, Shackleton House, 4 Battle Bridge Lane, London, SE1 2HX (www.cla.co.uk). Applications for the copyright owner's written permission should be addressed to the publisher.

Edited by Shelly Lyons
Designed by Bobbie Nuyton
Picture research by Jo Miller
Production by Katy LaVigne
Originated by Capstone Global Library Ltd

ISBN 978 1 3982 0229 0 (hardback)
ISBN 978 1 3982 0230 6 (paperback)

British Library Cataloguing in Publication Data
A full catalogue record for this book is available from the British Library.

Acknowledgements
Getty Images: Brian J. Skerry, 10; Shutterstock: Adrian Hughes, 8, Altrendo Images, 5, Andrea Izzotti, 3, Andrey Novgorodtsev, 6, apple2499, Cover, BMJ, 21, dangdumrong, 25, daniiD, 7, Darren Baker, 29, 30, Dennis Jacobsen, 15, dirkr, 28, Jan Martin Will, 17, Joe McDonald, 13, 14, Johan C. op den Dries, 23, Johan Swanepoel, 27, Landshark1, 26, Marina Demkina, 16, Menno Schaefer, 22, MZPHOTO.CZ, 18, Olga Bogatyrenko, 20, PRILL, 24, Richard Constantinoff, 19, Sermsak S, 4, shymar27, 11, Tom Tietz, 12, wildestanimal, 9

Design Elements
Capstone; Shutterstock: Artishok, cajoer, Fourleaflover, linear_design, srikorn thamniyom

Printed and bound in India.

Well done! Try all the books in this series!